THE SEASIDE HOUSE

NICK VOULGARIS III PHOTOGRAPHS BY DOUGLAS FRIEDMAN
FOREWORD BY MARTHA STEWART

LIVING ON THE WATER

RIZZOLI
NEW YORK

New York · Paris · London · Milan

First published in the United States of America in 2017
by Rizzoli International Publications, Inc.
300 Park Avenue South
New York, NY 10010
www.rizzoliusa.com

2017 2018 2019 2020 / 10 9 8 7 6 5 4 3 2 1

Distributed to the U.S. trade by Random House, New York

Design by Claudia Brandenburg, Language Arts

Printed in China

ISBN-13: 978-0-8478-5836-1

Library of Congress Control Number: 2016956148

FOREWORD

Nick Voulgaris and Douglas Friedman are an inimitable team. Together they have compiled a beautiful and inspiring book: Nick has written carefully researched text about a group of well-chosen homes that are on or within view of water. Douglas, with his personable talent, has photographed these properties, revealing rooms that are perfect for their location and usage, with views that are gorgeous and memorable. Each home is located either on the east or west coast or in the Caribbean, and each displays a fine attention to "place" or location, with interesting architecture, wonderful design, and lovely decoration and landscape.

Living on the water is a very personal choice for homeowners, and despite the fact that there are no people in the photographs, one enjoys the images with a real feeling of getting to know the inhabitants of the homes in the book. And even if you have never thought of living in close proximity to water—or are not been lucky enough to have bought a piece of real estate on the shore of an ocean, a lake, a river, or a pond—this book will make you rethink your living choices and possibly encourage you to think again about where you will reside.

I have been fortunate to work for years in an office with an amazing view of the adjacent Hudson River, and my daughter lives with her children in a building with a similar, ever changing, exciting view in downtown Manhattan. In northern Maine, my home looks out over the coast, the ocean peppered with islands, alive with weather, and birds and sea life. I have come to love seeing the water, experiencing the varied landscapes, and the myriad activities that take place on the seascape, and I would not want to give that up for some other place. After you peruse the images in this book and read the stories of each home, I think you, too, will be drawn to looking for "The Seaside House."

Martha Stewart

INTRODUCTION

I have been drawn to the water for as long as I can remember. Ever since I was whisked aboard my parents' thirty-foot wooden sailboat at the tender age of three months, the desire to be near the water has been a constant in my life.

I seek solace at the waterfront. I find the sea calming and restorative, as it allows me to reflect on the simplicity of life. The broad expanse of the ocean reminds me of the vastness of our world and can quickly put any problem I am facing into perspective. And yet the intimacy and peacefulness of a small bay or tidal marsh makes me feel ensconced and safe, protected by the shore and sea grass that surround me.

I find the cool, briny aroma of saltwater intoxicating. Growing up surrounded by water in Long Island, I spent summers sailing on small boats, water skiing, digging for clams, setting lobster traps, or playing in the mud flats at low tide. Almost every weekend we would explore a new harbor on our family's cruising sailboat. The excitement of arriving in a new port was palpable, and my brother and I could not wait to jump into the dinghy and head to the beach. We would collect beach glass with my mother, and later go crabbing with my father.

The highlight of every summer was spending the month of August living aboard the boat.

We would cruise eastern Long Island Sound, Rhode Island, and Cape Cod. By the age of five or six, I had already been introduced to such enchanting places as Shelter Island, Block Island, Newport, Nantucket, and Martha's Vineyard. Time seemed to move more slowly back then, and it felt like we spent an eternity exploring the harbors and small villages. I can still hear the sounds of the foghorn coming from the lighthouse in Nantucket, and the clickity-clack of automobiles driving over the centuries-old cobblestone streets of Martha's Vineyard. This was a magical time in my life, and I look back on it with the fondest of memories.

Since then, being near the water has become a need for me, as it has for the homeowners in this book. There is something powerful about living by the sea, being so close to its large waves and unimaginable depths. But there is comfort, too, in the soothing sounds, the predictability of the tides, and the gentle movement of the water. I can gaze for hours at the flickering sunlight that dances in the small ripples of a lake, or endlessly daydream while looking at a harbor.

My love for the sea inspired me to create a book that captures the essence of living on the water. I have collaborated with my friend, the celebrated photographer Douglas Friedman, who has perfectly encapsulated the character of each property by the sea, whether it's a rustic bungalow amid the sea grass on Long Island's east end, or a modern masterpiece overlooking the Pacific Ocean.

We chose properties with differing—and sometimes opposing—definitions of what it means to live on the water, whether in a glass and cement sculpture on a beach in Miami, a former fishing station on a Provincetown pier, or a swank retreat on a cliff in Antigua.

Each of the homeowners has his or her own connection to the sea— something that drew them to the shore in the first place and convinced them that they needed to stay. For many, the sea is restorative and calming.

Donna Karan designed her East Hampton abode with her late husband, artist Stephan Weiss, to be a Zen-like oasis by the water, away from the burdens and stresses of everyday life.

For others a seaside house is a place to indulge a love for the architecture and design of coastal communities. Perhaps it's affection for a place with a rich history, such as the homes of Steven Gambrel in Sag Harbor or Ken Fulk in Provincetown, or a desire for a modern house amid the rugged coastline, such as Donald Burns's Razor House in La Jolla.

Other homes in this book embody the lifestyle of a much simpler time, when families would gather in small cabins near the water and enjoy fishing, swimming, and sailing; such is the case of Elena Colombo's Greenport bungalow and the summer cottage in Shelter Island.

For many, being near the sea provides inspiration for their creative work. Fashion designer Elie Tahari finds creativity in time spent on the water at his Sagaponack summer house. And Martha Stewart's Seal Harbor compound is an open canvas to hone her many talents.

Living by the sea is truly an enchanting experience, filling the senses with its natural beauty, meditative sounds, and cool breezes. I hope this book will draw you into that special place, even if for just a few moments.

NANTUCKET MASSACHUSETTS

Off the southern coast of Cape Cod lies Nantucket, one of the best-preserved examples of early American history in a seaside town. The island ironically owes much of its preserved charm to the discovery of petroleum oil and the introduction of the combustion engine.

During the late 1600s, Nantucket was one of the top whaling ports of the northeast, even coined the "whaling capital of the world." This title remained for close to two hundred years as the island enjoyed immense prosperity. Whale blubber and oil were bought, sold, and refined in the town's bustling waterfront district. But by the mid-1800s the whaling industry was in decline, and its bounty was no longer desirable once petroleum became widely available.

Soon after, the town was ravaged by a fire—in part fueled by whale oil—that destroyed numerous buildings. Unable to earn a living or support themselves, island residents left and Nantucket was essentially abandoned. The result of this mass depopulation was an island preserved as if it were in a time capsule until the 1950s. At that time, preservationists and developers worked together to ensure that this special island would not lose its character as it would quickly became a summer destination for wealthy New Englanders.

Upon his first visit to Nantucket several decades ago, Donald Burns knew he would one day own a home there. He fell in love with the remote feeling and detachment of a community reachable only by ferry or plane. He wanted to be able to walk to the village for coffee and be part of the town's daily activity but also have enough property for privacy.

He was fortunate enough to hear about a four-acre subdivision that was purportedly going to be listed for sale. He made the owners an unsolicited offer and was able to purchase the property as one parcel, ensuring that all of the land would stay intact. This would later please the Nantucket Historic District Commission, which helped enable Mr. Burns to create the home that he envisioned.

He created a beautiful island retreat, designed by noted architect Hugh Newell Jacobsen, that masterfully blends Nantucket's historic fabric with a nod toward modernism. Although the home has tall, pitched roofs with dormers, it is only a single story. The result is a brilliantly bright and open interior with a dramatic spatial impact. The home's exterior features shakes of white cedar, which have weathered over time from the island's fog, salt air, and wind. A guest wing and pool are perfectly positioned to take full advantage of the harbor view.

PRECEDING
The exterior of this Nantucket home features white cedar shakes that have turned to a silvery gray color that pops against the crisp white trim.

RIGHT
With its clean lines and sleek new pool, the owner was able to create a modern home that still possesses the flavor of traditional Nantucket.

ABOVE
The main kitchen features
cabinetry and an island
finished in a high-gloss laminate
designed by Hugh Newell
Jacobsen and manufactured by
Woodmeister Master Builders.
The Hudson Furniture table
and bench, with brown leather
cushions, are made of solid
walnut.

RIGHT
The sophisticated dining room
contains a table and chairs
from Hermès. The stemware is
Baccarat and the rug is by Kyle
Bunting.

LEFT
The living room facing
Nantucket Harbor has reclaimed
teak floors that were salvaged
from a temple in Southeast Asia.
Custom windows and doors
are by Jacobsen Architecture,
including a guillotine window
in the center that slides upward
into the wall. The daybed is
by Mies van der Rohe, and the
cocktail tables are polished
sapphire glass with a "T" base
designed by the architect.

RIGHT
The simple, clean lines in the
bedroom do not distract from the
extraordinary view. The painting
over the mantel is by John Henry
Dolph, and the fireplace contains
selenite logs by Creel and Gow.

LEFT
Glass connections or "links" between each pavilion were conceived by architect Hugh Newell Jacobsen. The Nantucket Historic District Commission wanted the design to incorporate sloped roofs on top of the links but relented when they saw how beautifully the glass boxes interacted with the rest of the design.

RIGHT
The flagpole and lawn with a northeast view of Nantucket harbor and the Atlantic Ocean beyond.

GREENPORT
NEW YORK

Just past the vineyards on Long Island's North Fork, and at the very of the end of the Long Island Railroad, lies the quaint village of Greenport, New York. Like many coastal communities, Greenport's roots were in fishing and shipbuilding, due to its protected harbors, and its proximity to the open waters of Block Island Sound and the Atlantic Ocean. Over time those industries retreated, and, during prohibition, the village played host to rumrunners and speakeasies. Boats would shuttle the contraband in and out of town, and the restaurants would secretly serve it to those in the know.

Greenport was also home to a bustling brick factory that sat on a prime, west-facing waterfront parcel. In the early 1900s, the company built thirty-one small cottages for its workers. After the hurricane of 1938, the company closed, and the cottages were moved alongside the bay and eventually rented out.

Designer Elena Colombo was one of the lucky renters who purchased her cottage when all thirty-one units were sold as a cooperative, along with their ninety-acre lot, saving it from development. Her casual two-bedroom bungalow sits on the bay, with a separate sleeping porch and views of the dramatic sunsets.

The home has a comfortable, easy feel, with white-washed walls and painted wooden floors. To decorate her home, she was inspired by items that wash up on the beach and the colors from her garden. She likes things simple and unpretentious, and in fact has a rule of not spending more than one hundred dollars on any object or furnishing for the home. The focus instead is on being out in nature and taking in the view of the dramatic weather as it comes in across the water.

ABOVE
The rear facade of the cottage
has an attached potting shed and
outdoor shower just a few steps
from the bay.

RIGHT
Two vintage chairs were found
at Beall & Bell in Greenport.
The exposed beams of the
uninsulated walls make perfect
shelves. The chain art above
the window is made from metal
beer caps.

PRECEDING
A steel fire pit of Elena
Colombo's design and teak chairs
are perched on the water's edge
in Greenport.

LEFT
Sloped, painted wood floors
lead from the living room into
the master bedroom. The home,
built on locust posts, has settled
onto the beach, as there is no
foundation. The fireplace was
built from bricks made on site at
the former brick factory.

RIGHT
A small bench features a
driftwood lamp that the
owner found at the Cutchogue
recycling center, a collection of
porcupine quills, and a vintage
wine demijohn. The hearth
basket below stores kindling.
The silhouette on the wall was
purchased at a local flea market.

LEFT
Painted bead board lines the kitchen walls and ceiling. Note the "cupping" or raised edges of the light blue floor planks, a permanent reminder of storms that caused seawater to enter the home. The cast-iron farm sink and brass chandelier are original to the home. The cupboard over the stove is a medicine chest from a ship.

FOLLOWING, LEFT
The guest room is furnished with a cast-iron bed found in rural Pennsylvania. The night table contains a collection of vintage medicine bottles.

FOLLOWING, RIGHT
The bookshelves in the living room were built by the village mayor, who is also a craftsman. Painted tree stumps serve as stools, and a Chesapeake Bay oyster plate is displayed on the coffee table.

SOUTHAMPTON
NEW YORK

Southampton was settled in 1640, when a group of English Puritans left Lynn, Massachusetts, and landed on the shores of what is now known as Long Island. Named after the British Earl of Southampton, it is the oldest English settlement in the state of New York. The village is home to the Shinnecock Indian Reservation, the base of the Shinnecock Indian Nation. The village's rich history and oceanfront locale make it a popular destination for summer visitors and year-round residents alike.

Jane Holzer, a former model and Andy Warhol muse, sought a piece of property on the ocean where she could escape the trappings of New York City. Drawn to the water, she was looking for the quintessential "shack on the beach" that had style and beauty.

Her architect, the late Francis Fleetwood (known for creating classic cedar shake homes), found a modest oceanfront house in Southampton that he was quite sure would work. Holzer flew from Palm Beach to see the place and bought it immediately, knowing it would not last another day on the market.

Fleetwood adjusted the elevation of the home by raising the surrounding landscape one full story, then adding an additional story to the existing structure. This gave the renovated house better protection against storms as well as sweeping vistas of the Atlantic Ocean. Jane has decorated her home with vintage furniture that she has collected from around the world and numerous original works by Andy Warhol.

PRECEDING
The living room, facing the
Atlantic Ocean, is flooded with
light. The sofa on the left is
by Samuel Marx and the one
to the right is by Heywood-
Wakefield. The surfboard is by
Christopher Makos.

RIGHT
The grade of the land was raised
a full story to better protect
against storm surges. As a result,
the deck—with vintage Richard
Schultz furniture—offers an
enhanced view of the sea.

LEFT
A side deck for dining has 1950s Woodard furniture.

RIGHT
A sitting area in one of the living rooms features an original Andy Warhol series titled *Drag Queens*. The lamp was purchased at an auction, and the beige table is by Samuel Marx.

The owner wanted the furniture to be "drip dry" so her guests could sit down with wet bathing suits—hence the leather chaises. The chairs are by Paul T. Frankl, and the blankets are vintage Hermès.

The dining room is furnished with a modern glass table. The Wisteria dining chairs were once owned by Tennessee Williams. The Thomas Struth photograph was purchased because it so perfectly fits with the view out the adjacent window.

The idyllic pool, adorned
with white hydrangea trees,
was added by the owner.

SHELTER ISLAND
NEW YORK

Nestled between the north and south forks of
Eastern Long Island, Shelter Island is one of those
special places where time seems to stand still.
The island, insulated from the hustle and bustle of
the neighboring Hamptons, is only accessible by
boat or plane.

The owners of this home were first introduced
to the island decades earlier, when they would stay
aboard their friends' sailboat moored in Dering
Harbor. They would cruise Shelter Island Sound
and venture on trips to Block Island. After falling
in love with the island, they decided to rent a home
there and eventually bought a house in nearby
Shelter Island Heights.

One Sunday in February 1980, while reading the
Shelter Island Reporter, they saw a small classified
ad that read, "Victorian Cottage Facing Sunset on
Dering Harbor." Curious, they set up an appoint-
ment to see it. The couple was amazed to find that
the "cottage" was actually a very large house that
was directly on the water. They knew that this was
their chance to own a waterfront home, and if they
didn't act that day, it would be gone by Monday.

Homes on Dering Harbor are often under the
same ownership for fifty years or more, and as that
was the case here, the couple eagerly purchased
this property. At the time, they were considered
"kids" by the old guard. Today, almost forty years
later, they now are the self-proclaimed old guard.

Built in 1874, the house was one of the original summer cottages of the Manhanset Hotel, which was destroyed by a fire in 1910. Used only in the summer, the home sat upon locust posts without a foundation and was never winterized. Through the years, the couple added a proper foundation, a cellar, a heating system, and insulation, as well as a dock. They have raised their children here, and now their grandchildren come to spend the summer on the harbor. Summer living on Shelter Island is easy and restful. The family enjoys sailing their boat or taking in the view from the large screened porch.

PRECEDING
Originally part of the Manhanset Hotel, this summer cottage on Shelter Island has a private dock on Dering Harbor. There is a vintage Chris Craft at the dock, and the wooden sailboat in the foreground is a 1941 Herreshoff 12 ½, also known as a Doughdish. There is an active fleet of more than sixty of these boats in Dering Harbor.

RIGHT
The screened-in porch faces the harbor and the boats sailing by. The ornate cedar shake siding and gingerbread accents are typical of homes built on the island in the late 1800s.

ABOVE
The informal living room has a
fireplace at one end and large
windows overlooking the harbor
at the other. The shelves are full
of vintage nautical books and
navigational implements. A large
model of the owners' Hinckley
sailboat sits on the mantel.

RIGHT
Vintage privacy shutters in
the dining room diffuse the
bright sun when needed.
The antique chandelier and
ship's lantern on the table
were originally oil lamps.

LEFT
The all-season sunroom off the
kitchen features rattan furniture.
The owners' blue forty-two-foot
Hinckley Sou'wester sailboat,
Alice, can be seen in the harbor.
Alice sleeps six and becomes
an extension of the home
for houseguests when all the
bedrooms fill up.

ABOVE
The screened-in porch is
furnished with vintage wicker
chairs and a sofa from the
owners' previous home on
Shelter Island. A model of the
Herreshoff 12 ½ sits on the
side table.

LEFT
A small guest room features simple pine floors and wood-paneled walls and ceilings. The watercolors are by nineteenth-century marine painter Frederick Cozzens.

RIGHT
A model of a New York pilot schooner sits atop a nineteenth-century New England drop-leaf table. Most of the period furniture in the house is from the owner's childhood home in Marblehead, Massachusetts. A Dutch sailing scene from the 1800s hangs on the wall.

FIRE ISLAND PINES
NEW YORK

Fire Island is one of several barrier islands that run along Long Island's southern shore. It consists of a handful of small communities that locals and tourists have flocked to for generations during the warm summer months.

Part of the allure is that these communities are free of automobiles and only accessible by boat or ferry. Instead of streets, there are charming wooden boardwalks inches above the sand and sea grass, reminding us of a simpler time.

Fire Island Pines is one of these special communities, where just off the ferry dock is a corral for dozens of red wagons that are used to transport groceries and luggage.

Architect Carlos Otero restored this 1965 Horace Gifford home in the Pines over a two-year period. Gifford had designed and built this bungalow as his personal residence, and Carlos wanted to preserve the home's historical significance.

Carlos painstakingly restored the original cedar paneling, removing coats of stain that a previous owner had applied. He also designed and installed an elegant yet simple pool that is the focal point of the front entry courtyard. A roof deck was added to maximize the water view, and functional outdoor furniture was custom built out of mahogany.

Upon entry, guests are greeted with the aroma of cedar. The home has a relaxed vibe, decorated with modernist furniture, some of which was designed and built by Horace Gifford himself.

PRECEDING
The floor-through living room
has sliding glass walls on both
sides overlooking the pool in the
front and the outdoor seating
area on the rear deck. The yellow
magazine holder is from the
1960s, and the outdoor dining
set was custom built. The two
ceramic sculptures on the lower
left of the photograph, made by
Carlos Otero, were finished in
off-white speckled glaze.

RIGHT
The owners installed a new
swimming pool in the front
courtyard and added a small roof
deck. The white cedar exterior
siding was replaced to match the
original, and all interior siding
was sanded bare to remove
several coats of stain.

LEFT
The entry features a 1960s teak Scandinavian sideboard and white ink drawings from Vietnam.

RIGHT
Designed by Horace Gifford, the original built-in sofas have been reupholstered in charcoal linen. The rug is Morrocan, and the coffee tables were made from large bamboo dim sum steamers. A 1960s Scandinavian fireplace takes the chill out of the air during the cooler months.

LEFT
Tall ceilings and high windows bring abundant light into the renovated kitchen. New cabinets were designed to match the existing paneling, and honed granite countertops were installed. The black pendant lighting is by Artek.

RIGHT
The midcentury dining table is by Eero Saarinen, and the cane chairs are from the Czech Republic. The pendant light is by Louis Poulsen.

FOLLOWING, LEFT
The master bedroom features double-height ceilings, with all surfaces and window shades in white cedar. The geometric cotton bed cover was purchased from a market in Bangkok. The small benches used as night stands came with the purchase of the home.

FOLLOWING, RIGHT
This wooden boardwalk leads to the home, with the Great South Bay beyond. Fire Island, which does not accommodate cars, has miles of boardwalks.

MALIBU
CALIFORNIA

For those drawn to the sea, having a house on the water in Malibu is a dream come true. The stunning views and the ethereal sounds of the Pacific Ocean make it one of the most desirable waterfront communities to call home.

Located in southern California, Malibu has a temperate climate, beautiful beaches, and proximity to Hollywood, making it highly sought after for both celebrities and surfers alike. There are twenty-one miles of beautiful sandy beaches, most of which are open to the public.

Architect and designer Jamie Bush was given the task of designing the interiors and finishes for his client's home overlooking the ocean. Although the house had a modern overall design, Jamie incorporated visual and tactile textures to give the spaces a warmer feel. The goal was to design a home that would be comfortable and casual, while maximizing the view of the Pacific Ocean and the beaches below.

The color selection throughout reflects the muted palette of seaside living, with inspiration taken from sand and driftwood. Some of floors are planked with travertine tile, and, to define different spaces, the walls transition from a smooth white to a gray-washed board and batten with a ceruse finish that brings out the grain.

There is a seamless flow from the indoor spaces onto the deck, thanks to a glass wall that disappears. The interior travertine floors seem to blend perfectly onto the teak deck that is cantilevered over the hill. Glass and metal rails that define the outdoor spaces ensure an unobstructed view of the sea below.

PRECEDING
Centered in the living room is a
custom bleached coffee table by
Stefan Bishop that complements
the natural hues of the silver
travertine plank floors and
cerused white oak ceiling. A
large sofa and ottomans provide
seating. The "Circle Chair" in the
corner is by Hans Wegner.

RIGHT
The kitchen has a disappearing
wall that opens to the outdoor
deck and views of the Pacific
Ocean. The oak cabinetry is
finished with a gray stain, and
the countertops are granite.
Outside is a teak sectional sofa
and large sea sponges from Dao.

LEFT
The free-form dining table is constructed of Australian acacia wood, with chairs by Rodolfo Dordoni. The floors are silver travertine plank, and the bronze and copper chandelier is by Christopher Boots. The mirror is from the designer's own line, Jamie Bush & Co.

ABOVE
The master bedroom has breathtaking views of the Malibu beach and ocean, with disappearing walls that open to the deck. The floors are white oak, and the rug is Moroccan. The designer conceived the custom floating nightstands and a built-in bed of gray oak and leather. The vintage lounge chair is by Hans Wegner.

FOLLOWING, LEFT
The office has access to the deck and an inspiring view of the ocean. A light fixture by Verner Panton and a driftwood mobile hang from the ceiling.

FOLLOWING, RIGHT
The wing chair in the corner of the dining room is a "Star Trek Special Edition" by Ceccotti. The weathered cast stone chair on the deck is by Dessin Fournir.

BLOCK ISLAND
RHODE ISLAND

Block Island has a windswept topography, with low-lying shrubs and masterfully built stone walls that date back to the 1600s. Its accessibility only by sea or air adds to its allure and mystique.

Most of the buildings on the island are of cedar shake construction and have gracefully aged to a gray patina from the perfect combination of salt air and wind. The island's rolling hills, endless nature trails, and seventeen miles of unspoiled shoreline complete the fantasy of this very special place.

Chuck and Jill Townsend were enjoying an afternoon aboard their boat *Island Girl* in Block Island's Great Salt Pond when they noticed a classified advertisement in the *Block Island Times* for a small house on the pond's northern shore. Chuck had been visiting Block Island for over thirty years and was quickly able to identify the home from their boat. They called the broker immediately, and the rest is history.

Over the next two years, the couple oversaw the transformation of the poorly conceived structure, essentially rebuilding the whole house from the slab up. Jill's father, a mason, installed a beautiful stone fireplace that anchors the living room. Their love for the sea and sailing is evident with nautical touches, mahogany wood trim, and to-die-for views facing both south to the Great Salt Pond and north to Rhode Island.

PRECEDING
The owner's classic Jeep Grand
Wagoneer is parked on the
lawn with the island's harbor,
the Great Salt Pond, in the
background. The Great Salt Pond
was originally that—a large
pond—until a channel was dug
in 1895 to connect the body of
water to Block Island Sound.

RIGHT
The sitting room furniture is
adorned with nautical code
flag pillows. The coffee table is
stacked with books about sailing
and the sea.

LEFT
The kitchen features Carrera marble countertops and panoramic views of the sand dunes, harbor, and sound.

RIGHT
The seating area in the kitchen features a banquette and Lister Teak chairs from a previous yacht that the couple had owned.

LEFT
The owners found this hand-painted table and chairs in a shop on Nantucket. A painting of their classic 1956 Sparkman & Stevens yawl FIDELIO hangs on the wall.

ABOVE
Block Island is known for its miles of hand-built stone walls that date back to the 1600s, when they were used to mark property lines and contain livestock. The rolling dunes and ocean can be seen in the distance.

The master bedroom has stunning views of the salt marsh and the Great Salt Pond. An alcove to the right features a writing desk and binoculars for watching the boats coming in to port.

NEWPORT
RHODE ISLAND

Located on Aquidneck Island, Newport has a storied history along its waterfront that includes shipbuilding, whaling, piracy, and most recently, yachting. Newport has long been a summer haven for residents from New York and Philadelphia, among others, who built immense summer "cottages" for entertaining in grand style during the Gilded Age of the late 1800s and early 1900s.

Such prominent families as the Astors, Vanderbilts, and Dukes owned houses along Bellevue Avenue and called Newport home during the summer months. Although a good number of the original mansions no longer exist, many of them have been preserved.

Beaulieu is one those homes. A stately residence, it was designed by Calvert Vaux and built in 1862 for the Peruvian ambassador to the U.S. The formal gardens that overlook the sea were created by Frederick Law Olmstead.

Wiley and Ruth Buchanan purchased Beaulieu in 1961, and it has been in their family ever since. The house was abandoned when they bought it, stripped of its marble mantels, doorknobs, chandeliers, and sconces. The Buchanans traveled to Europe to replace many of the missing items, and designer Valerian Rybar conceived the interiors for the young family. They had been impeccably preserved by Mrs. Buchanan through the years and remain unchanged, largely due to her insistence that all the furniture, art, and window treatments are properly covered with sheets each winter.

One of the Buchanans' children, Dede, fondly recalls how her late father would say "come sit in my office with me," as he gestured to an empty chair next to his on the terrace overlooking the ocean. Together they would enjoy an expansive view of the Atlantic from this spot, perched high along the cliffs in Newport.

PRECEDING
The slate terrace faces the Atlantic Ocean. Below the balustrade at the edge of the lawn is Newport's fabled cliff walk.

RIGHT
A side view of the entry foyer. The exquisite paneling detail is original to the home, as are the bronze banister and marble floors. The owners found the chandelier on a trip to Europe.

ABOVE
The simple, efficient kitchen
has not changed since the owner
renovated it in 1961. The cabinets
are painted metal, and the floor
is Linoleum.

RIGHT
The breakfast room, like most
of the house, is original to the
1961 design of Valerian Rybar.
The perimeter of the nook
features custom-built mirrored
planters beneath the windows.
Bronze hands holding lamps
serve as sconces.

A cutting garden and privet hedge with archway lead to the lawn overlooking the bay. The family's Chevrolet Caprice Classic station wagon has been in active service for decades.

LEFT
A sitting area in a guest room has yellow and coral accents and orange flowered wallpaper. Mrs. Buchanan felt that some of the flowers ought to be pink, so she climbed up a ladder and painted them by hand.

RIGHT
One of the most utilized rooms in the house is the parlor, with a card table that is often used for the game Spite and Malice. The oil landscape hanging to the left is by Jean Dufy, and the portrait on the right is the work of Mary Cassatt.

When the home was first built,
this room served as the man's
master bedroom, back when
couples did not share a room.
Today it is a dressing room
and study.

DOMINICAN REPUBLIC

Located in the Caribbean, on the eastern side of the island of Hispaniola, is the Dominican Republic, with its blue waters, white sandy beaches, and smaller offshore islands and cays. A short walk inland is farmland, tall mountains, and a deep jungle.

Designer Celerie Kemble and her husband, along with a group of friends, set out to find an idyllic spot on the island to build private homes around a central meeting place where they could vacation together.

On the northern side of the island, nestled in between the villages of Cabrera and Rio San Juan, they found a spectacular waterfront site with a beach, just at the foot of the mountains.

They transformed the site into a private oasis where they could all gather during vacations, while having the ability to retreat to their individual homes. Celerie designed the homes and clubhouse with an "old Victorian–Palm Beach" aesthetic. She re-created the triple-gable roofline from her grandparents' kit house that she remembers as a child growing up in Palm Beach.

The spirit and whimsy of the new structures fit perfectly among the rugged mountains, sandy beach, and ocean. Celerie chose easy beach colors and comfortable furnishings with a worn feeling. The goal was to make each home feel like it has been there for decades. Floors are made from concrete tile, and a local ironworker was commissioned to build the iron gates and metal chandeliers. Wooden *tragaluz* cutouts over the doors and windows give the interior architecture a traditional Spanish feel, while letting in streaks of light and glimpses of blue sea.

PRECEDING
The exterior of this triple-gable Victorian was designed by the owner to resemble her family's original kit home in Palm Beach. There are intricate wooden details on the fascia, railings, and window trim. The roof is painted metal.

RIGHT
The bright, airy living room features green chairs from the designer's collection for Henredon and a vintage Paul Frankl sofa. *Tragaluz* details in the wooden panels over the doorways were designed by Kemble and inspired by Elric Elersby's collection of historic patterns. The custom copper palm frond ceiling lights were made by a local ironworker.

LEFT
The seating area in the gazebo room has vintage wicker chairs and a rattan sofa. The floors are constructed of handmade octagonal concrete tile, and the walls are *tabla de palma*, a royal palm wood material used extensively on the island.

RIGHT
The *tragaluz* detail over the doorways, enhanced by copper palm frond accents, continues into the kitchen, with its large copper farm sink. A vintage wicker watermelon picnic basket awaits an adventure to the beach.

LEFT
The clubhouse's porch bar features custom iron and copper rocking chairs modeled on French vintage pieces. Royal palm wood paneling that has been painted and distressed covers the exterior walls, and the floor is ipe.

RIGHT
The seating area of the bar has a vintage Crespi cane and bamboo sofa covered with a mix of Dutch African wax print cushions and pillows with ikats and Uzbeki embroideries. The ceiling fixture is a collection of copper stars.

ABOVE
The master bedroom's dramatic
tray ceiling features hand-carved
panels and copper lighting. The
custom bed is upholstered in
raffia. A seating area consists of
faux bois chairs and a ceramic
garden stool. Floors are painted a
pale mint color.

RIGHT
The master bathroom features
a large copper soaking tub. The
vanity was inspired by vintage
garden planters custom made
in the Dominican Republic. The
walls are bead board, and
the ceiling is painted a pale
aqua color.

The pool and cabanas
overlooking the sea reflect
designer Celerie Kemble's
influence from Victorian
Palm Beach.

SAGAPONACK NEW YORK

Sagaponack, a small village in the Town of Southampton, was first settled in the mid-1600s, predominantly for farming potatoes. Originally called Sagg, the village later adopted the Shinnecock Indian name Sagaponack, which means "large ground nut." Its desirable location along the Atlantic Ocean later made Sagaponack a popular summer destination, drawing writers, celebrities, bankers, and politicians.

Fashion designer Elie Tahari bought a home on the Sagaponack beach named Crestview. Built in the 1800s as a barn in Vermont, it had been completely disassembled and moved to its current site, where the structure was transformed into a home that blends the rustic barn aesthetic with clean, modern finishes.

Tall, cathedral ceilings reveal the original barn's exposed beams and allow an expansive, airy feel. Walls of glass let in light, and an enormous garage door opens up to the ocean and the sounds of the sea. The home has a truly private oceanfront beach, as well as a large aqua lap pool nestled under trees.

Mr. Tahari's home is a sanctuary: a place where he and his family go to rest and relax. But the home also stimulates his creativity, as being on the water inspires his work. It's not surprising that many of the designs for his fashion line are conceived at this blissful place near the sea.

PRECEDING
The swimming pool at the home
of Elie Tahari is surrounded
by landscaping designed by
Edwina von Gal.

RIGHT
A massive raised glass wall
provides a view from the main
living space to the garden.

LEFT
The 1800s barn has been converted to a home by Elie Tahari, with interior design by Tom Flynn.

RIGHT
A seating area in the living room has rattan armchairs and a vintage Herman Miller coffee table.

LEFT
The dining table is by Joseph D'Urso, and the chairs are vintage. Art by Deborah Kass and Elliott Puckette hangs above the stairs and dining table.

RIGHT
A corner sitting area with a Grasshopper chaise in steel and leather designed in 1968 by Preben Fabricius and Jorgen Kastholm. The photograph is from the *Horseplay* series by David LaChapelle featuring Angelina Jolie. The bag is from Elie Tahari's collection.

PROVINCETOWN MASSACHUSETTS

It has been said it's the light that attracts painters, and the quiet peacefulness of being by the sea that draws in authors and poets. Whatever the reason, Provincetown, which was initially a fishing port, has become a haven for artists and creative types, including Tennessee Williams, Jackson Pollock, and Michael Cunningham. This small, seaside town is a whimsical place on the tip of Cape Cod where drag queens, sea captains, artists, and designers live in harmony.

Designer Ken Fulk, who calls Provincetown "magical," spotted an old, ramshackle home that sat right on the water's edge and decided to approach the owner about selling it. The two were unable to reach a deal just then, but four years later, fate intervened and Ken purchased the home.

Although it was in need of substantial repairs, the house had wonderful character, and Ken wanted to retain its historical integrity. He decided not to refinish the floors, instead opting to have them scrubbed and cleaned and patched where needed. Any paint that was falling off the walls was removed, but the rest was just washed and the original wallpaper preserved. Even the room numbers remain on each of the bedroom doors from the days when this home was a boardinghouse.

Ken, who typically works with a large team for his clients' installations, handpicked every piece of furniture and placed each piece of art for this home. The result of his substantial preservation efforts is a seaside home that exudes authentic charm and character, with a mélange of aged colors.

The rear of the home faces
the bay, with a large deck and
pier. The cedar shakes on this
elevation, damaged by harsh
wind and saltwater, were
replaced during the renovation.

RIGHT
The front parlors are furnished
with finds from around the
world, including a nineteenth-
century English sofa that has
been reupholstered in a Ralph
Lauren plaid fabric, and an
Italian fantasy chair with its
original pink velvet, now worn.
The globe is from a German
cruise ship.

LEFT
The canopy bed in a guest room is from "Topridge," Marjorie Merriweather Post's camp in the Adirondacks. The aged painted plaster walls were left in their natural state wherever possible throughout the home.

ABOVE
The dining room features a hand-painted mural of historic Provincetown by Rafael Arana. English chairs with individual needlepoint seats surround a nineteenth-century gate-leg captain's table.

LEFT
The kitchen was restored with simple Shaker-style cabinets and butcher-block counters. An original Chambers stove was installed, and an old utility tub was put into service as an extra-deep kitchen sink.

RIGHT
Antique copper pots hang above a butcher's block in the pantry.

LEFT
The front entry hall and staircase are more elaborate and grand than most found in Provincetown. The campaign chest was found at the Brimfield Antique Show, and the walls are decorated with a collection of vintage portraits.

RIGHT
The master bath, with period sinks and a claw-foot tub, encompasses what was originally a smaller adjacent bedroom, one of the few alterations made to the original house.

LEFT
The library is painted a curry color that glows in the morning sun as well as in the evening, lit only by the fireplace. A nineteenth-century brass captain's bed is used for reading or additional guest quarters.

RIGHT
The "captain's room" has a nineteenth-century Windsor chair and a pair of vintage nautical paintings with original rope frames. Simple linen panels attached to iron hooks serve as drapes.

FOLLOWING, LEFT
The enclosed sun porch, with the original blue painted floors, is furnished with an antique bridge table and a set of primitive nineteenth-century chairs. When the home was acquired, the porch was held up by a car jack, which was eventually replaced by a proper foundation.

FOLLOWING, RIGHT
One of the many porches, with a view of the harbor through the library door. The quartet of rocking chairs faces west, toward the afternoon sun.

PROVINCETOWN MASSACHUSETTS

Provincetown is a meeting ground for creative types, which is precisely what attracted the owners of this waterfront cabin to the charming seaside town. Decades earlier, they had visited Captain Jack's Wharf and took notice of the quaint fishing station that was converted into residences on a long pier. So when the opportunity came to purchase one of the cabins, they were ready.

The wharf and its small cabins were built in the late 1800s for fishermen to store their tackle and sell fish. And in later years, this became a place for artists to gather. It was not uncommon to spot Tennessee Williams or Eugene O'Neill on the wharf during the 1940s.

This particular unit, the last one on the pier, has water on three sides. At high tide you can hear the water lapping under the floorboards. When the owners purchased the cabin, it had sat empty for a number of years and needed minor updating. Fortunately, the cabin had great bones, needing only cosmetic upgrades and decorating.

Since the floorboards often get wet from the water below, the edges of the planks became cupped through the years. The owners sanded down the high edges of the floor, revealing layers of different colored paint that they preserved by coating it with polyurethane. They wanted to maintain the cabin's salty, boathouse feel and give it a timeless aesthetic. Aside from painting surfaces, they only updated the kitchen and bathroom.

The soaring, open ceiling remains as it was over one hundred years ago. And the large rope-and-pulley-operated window, which was designed for selling fish, now is used to open up the cabin to the sea that surrounds it.

PRECEDING
The cottage's sliding barn-style
doors open up the living room
to the sea. Cedar Adirondack
chairs and chaise longues on the
pier outside are for taking in
the view.

RIGHT
A 1930s rattan sofa from L.A.
and worn 1940s French leather
club chairs anchor the living
room. To the left is the large
window originally used
for selling fish, and above
the kitchen is the guest loft.

LEFT
The crisp white walls and
exposed ceiling beams of the
cabin are the backdrop for
an open kitchen with zinc
countertops. The dining area
features an oak and wicker table
that the owners found in Maine.
A comfortable window seat looks
out to the bay. The high spots
of the original wood floors were
sanded flat to reveal numerous
colors beneath.

ABOVE
In the master bedroom, a vintage
hutch is centered between two
windows with original working
privacy shutters.

A nineteenth-century American flag hangs on the wood-paneled wall of the master bedroom. Flanking the king-size bed are contemporary side tables made from reclaimed driftwood.

EAST HAMPTON
NEW YORK

On the south fork of Long Island lies East Hampton, bordered by the Atlantic Ocean to the south and Gardiner's Bay to the north. East Hampton's roots are steeped in farming and whaling. Today the village is known for its sandy beaches, chic boutiques, and private estates.

Designer Donna Karan and her late husband, Stephan, had been summering on Fire Island for years when they decided to purchase a home in East Hampton. After settling into what they called the White House, the place next door became available and they purchased it to create a spa-like retreat where Donna could practice yoga and rejuvenate.

The house had small, dark rooms and needed to be completely gutted. Donna craved vast, open spaces and a seamless transition from the inside to the outside. She was inspired by the openness and connection to nature of Bali, her favorite place in the world.

The couple enlisted the architecture firm Spector Group and interior designer Bonetti/Kozerski. The result is a tranquil retreat with beautiful white rooms and natural tones that feel at one with nature and the water. The lower level features a yoga studio, spa, and outdoor stone shower. On the second level is one bedroom, a large master suite that Donna uses herself. Guests now sleep in the main house.

As with any renovation, mistakes were made: the sliding doors came in too short, and there is a small step up between the house and the deck. To this day, every time she stubs her toe, she looks up and smiles at Stephan.

The home is Donna's sanctuary. Her creative work is stimulated by living on the sea, with color and texture palettes inspired by her long walks on the beach.

PRECEDING
The view of the Atlantic
Ocean from Donna Karan's
East Hampton home.

LEFT
A large palm-wood bowl from
Bali and a reed basket from
Donna's Urban Zen collection
are placed beside a modern
fireplace.

RIGHT
A palatte of natural tones in
the living room includes white
surfaces and wood hues. The
chair and coffee table were
carved with a chainsaw.

LEFT
A collection of wooden and stone eggs adorns the dining room. The table and chairs are from Urban Zen.

RIGHT
The kitchen has clean lines, open shelves, and white surfaces. Countertops were made from cast white concrete. The antique stool is walnut.

LEFT
The bedroom floors are made
from reclaimed oak planks that
were bleached and finished with
oil. The bed was designed by
Bonetti/Kozerski and built of
reclaimed solid teak planks.

RIGHT
The master bathroom features
natural plaster-finished walls
and a custom sink made from
reclaimed Jerusalem limestone.
The mirror is salvaged, and the
parchment light fixture is by
Bonetti/Kozerski.

FLANDERS
NEW YORK

Flanders is a small cottage community along the western shores of Peconic Bay, within the town of Southampton, New York. In the early 1900s it served as a summer destination, with hotels and boarding houses that catered to the stage and carriage trades. A private sporting club was built, and the area enjoyed modest prosperity for several decades.

The Great Depression and World War II left Flanders empty and somewhat deserted. It would be years before the town would slowly rebuild and attract new residents. But eventually Flanders experienced an influx of veterans and their families, and later artists from New York City who were looking for a small bungalow near the bay during the summer months.

Photographer Dean Isidro learned about Flanders from his friend, designer Anthony Baratta, who owned a home there in a small enclave of cottages along the water. Anthony had heard that one of his neighbors was going to put his home on the market in a few days and mentioned it to Dean. Not wanting to miss the opportunity, Dean drove out to the house, parked in the driveway, and waited for the owner to come home from work to make an offer. The house would soon be his.

The house was in close to original condition, and he wanted to keep its simple, functional design intact. The group of bungalows was never meant for year-round living when they were built, so subsequent owners had to add insulation and heating systems for the winter months.

Dean opened up the ceilings, giving the home more height and interior light, and added fresh white paint to the walls. He restored the original floors, added new cedar shingles to the exterior, and built a pool. The quiet tranquility of the views over the salt marsh and Peconic Bay provide a gentle retreat from the realities of everyday life.

PRECEDING
The view of Peconic Bay.
Flanders is famous for the Big
Duck, a roadside attraction
pictured on the beach towels.

RIGHT
The cozy living room has a
stone fireplace and an Eames
chair. The owner purchased
the zebra rug while on a photo
shoot in Zambia. The balloon dog
sculpture is by Jeff Koons.

LEFT
Striped walls and an American flag blanket accent the guest room. The owner of the home is a car buff, as evidenced by the artwork over the bed. The nickel and glass side table is from Aero Studios, with a glass lamp by John Saladino.

RIGHT
The guest bedroom's Moroccan rug was purchased during a location shoot abroad. A tote bag hanging from the doorknob is for guests to take to the beach.

LEFT
The cottage is part of a small community where friends and neighbors frequently stop by. The front door has a "Y" or "N" to indicate whether or not the home is open to visitors. A vintage Mercedes sedan is used for trips to the market.

RIGHT
A quiet sitting area in the sunroom is stacked with wood for the fireplace. The owner found the 1950s bentwood chair on the streets of New York City.

LEFT
The original 1950s awning
windows in the sunroom face the
Peconic Bay. The dining table
is by Jeff Stern, and the Harry
Bertoia chairs were found at a
store on Long Island's North
Fork. The blue bowls are vintage
Pyrex, and the wood floor is
painted a faded blue-gray color.

ABOVE
The narrow 1950s aqua metal
secretary is used for occasional
work and writing letters.

LA JOLLA
CALIFORNIA

Nestled among the hills and cliffs of San Diego, California, lies the seaside community of La Jolla, with over seven miles of bluffs and sandy beaches. Journalist and publisher Ellen Browning Scripps made La Jolla her home in the early 1900s and used her wealth and influence to shape the town's architecture and culture. She personally commissioned numerous buildings, including the La Jolla Women's Club and the Scripps Institution of Oceanography. Her own residence is now the San Diego Museum of Contemporary Art.

Within La Jolla lies the Torrey Pines State Natural Reserve, a two-thousand-acre state park comprised of breathtaking cliffs and ocean bluffs that sit high above the Pacific Ocean. A large lagoon in the preserve is home to abundant wildlife and flora.

The Razor House was smartly built into a site on a cliff that originally was deemed unsuitable for building. The design and layout capture the expansive view of the ocean, as well as the texture and vibrancy of the preserve below.

Its smooth, white Portland cement walls and vast, open spaces give the house the feel of an art gallery, where both the structure and the view are the canvas. Part of the intrigue of the home is its floor-to-ceiling glass curtains and massive concrete walls, ceilings, and floors.

The texture of most poured concrete homes is marred with grain and imperfections from the plywood forms used to set the concrete. This is not the case with the Razor House, as all the wooden forms were coated with a smooth fiberglass resin, creating a finish surface resembling Venetian plaster.

Its current owner refers to the property as a sculpture rather than a house. When businessman Don Burns bought the home recently, it was still unfinished by the original owner, creating a unique opportunity to add intimate living spaces without compromising the original form of the house.

The home, designed by architect Wallace Cunningham, could be a case study in both engineering and art form. When Cunningham conceived the house, his choice of materials and the view from the building site were the driving factors in its design. He wanted to communicate both a permanence and sense of infinity. The sunbeams, shadows, reflections, and varying shades of the ocean make this residence a spectacular statement in seaside living.

PRECEDING
The home's infinity pool appears to flow into the sea. The ocean bluffs and Black's Beach are below; guest parking and guest quarters are above.

RIGHT
The curved glass wall of the living room looks out to the Pacific Ocean. The low-back chairs were designed to not obstruct the view and complement the custom Chester Moon sofa and Vietri coffee table by Baxter. The hanging stainless-steel floor speakers are by Garvan.

ABOVE
The central courtyard has a a
three-tiered terrace. Skylights
illuminate the garage below.
The stepping monolith walls
follow the hillside and the
driveway, culminating in a
celestial opening of the guest
house. To the right is the covered
breezeway of the pool with a
transparent guest suite above.

RIGHT
The eastern elevation of the
home on the left showcases the
curved walls of the bedroom,
with the living room below at
pool level. To the right is the
massive three-story Portland
cement wall, which was poured
in place during construction.
Farther right is the courtyard,
family room, and library, with a
belowground garage underneath.

LEFT
The family room, with views of
the pool and ocean, features a
large custom leather sofa and
green suede chairs by Baxter. To
the right is a linear gas fireplace
housed in a black granite plinth.
Above the black walnut ceiling is
the mezzanine library.

ABOVE
Curved stone stairs lead to the
master bath, with a large soaking
tub and vanity.

Called the "bridge," this guest suite and study has glass on both sides, offering views through the room from other areas of the house. The frameless windows pivot open in the glass curtain wall, and there is a private balcony. For privacy, the window coverings lower, creating an intimate bedroom. The bed and night stands are by Molteni.

MIAMI
FLORIDA

With its blue-green water, white-sand beaches, palm trees, and temperate climate, Miami is an ideal escape from the cold weather and snow of the Northeast. For Tommy Hilfiger and his wife, Dee, Miami was a perfect place to create a vacation home for friends and family members, close to their newly acquired Raleigh Hotel. It also provided a space to display their modern art collection, including important work by Andy Warhol, Jean-Michel Basquiat, Keith Haring, and Damien Hirst.

The couple purchased the 14,000-square-foot contemporary house on Golden Beach, one of the few Miami neighborhoods where they could find a single-family residence directly on the beach. They were attracted to its vast spaces and tall ceilings that emulated an art gallery—perfect for their contemporary collection. They enlisted designer Martyn Lawrence Bullard to help create a comfortable home for their family, where they could properly display their art.

Tommy and Dee wanted the home to be a departure from the traditional design of their Manhattan apartment at the Plaza Hotel and their country house in Greenwich, Connecticut. They envisioned the decor as "shagadelic and groovy," with overtones of 1960s and '70s disco fever. Martyn accomplished this by using bold colors, shag rugs, Lucite, and vintage furniture.

For the couple and their family, being on the water is magical: peaceful when the seas are calm; exciting and inspiring when the waves start to crash.

PRECEDING
The rear of this Miami home
owned by Tommy and
Dee Hilfiger faces the ocean.
A Keith Haring sculpture
presides over the pool.

RIGHT
The living room features a
colorful Kyle Bunting rug
designed by Martyn Lawrence
Bullard and sofas by Vladimir
Kagan. The vintage cocktail
table is by JF Chen.

ABOVE
The bedroom features a vintage
sofa and a Willy Rizzo coffee
table that opens up to reveal a
built-in bar. The bed is vintage
Paul Evans, and the photographs
are of the final Marilyn Monroe
shoot by Bert Stern.

LEFT
A sitting area is furnished with a
sofa by Martyn Lawrence Bullard
and chairs by Vladimir Kagan.
The art is by Andy Warhol.

A large 1970s disco ball sourced from a club in Capri hangs above the bar. Tracey Emin neon art graces the wall.

ABOVE
A view of the pool, paved in travertine by Ann Sacks, and the captivating blue water of the Atlantic Ocean. The deck furniture is by Richard Schultz for Knoll.

RIGHT
The kitchen has a breakfast table by Willy Rizzo with vintage chairs from JF Chen. The rendering of Elizabeth Taylor is by artist Vik Muniz.

FOLLOWING, LEFT
The kids' bathroom features scented banana wallpaper.

FOLLOWING, RIGHT
A children's room painted with red and white stripes features a Mickey Mouse print by Andy Warhol. The bed is upholstered with fabric by Manuel Canovas.

SAG HARBOR
NEW YORK

Located on Long Island's east end, Sag Harbor is rich in history from its early days as a whaling port and, after the fall of the whaling industry, home to a cotton mill, which eventually became the noted Watchcase factory. Sag Harbor is mentioned numerous times on the pages of *Moby-Dick*, and more recently, became the residence of noted writers John Steinbeck and William Demby.

Ship captains built their homes on Main Street, a safe distance from the chaos of the busy waterfront and smell of whale processing. The success of a whaling captain was often measured by the size of the home he built. A captain's home typically would start with the front facade bearing a door and two windows—known as a "half house." If an expedition went well, another wing was added, with two more windows on the opposite side to make a "full house." If expeditions continued to be lucrative, sometimes a second story would be added to create a center hall colonial.

Designer and architect Steven Gambrel bought this waterfront Sag Harbor home after living in the house across the street for many years. At the time, his puppy, Dash, would wander across his neighbor's lawn to the bay and refuse to come home. Steven soon realized that both he and Dash wanted a place on the water.

The house, built in the early 1800s, is an example of numerous additions from successful whaling expeditions. Steven put his talent to work to create a homogenous space that flows through each of the wings. The home can be both intimate for a couple and host to dinner for forty. Steven's classic Beetlecat sailboat and mahogany Hacker-Craft sit at the dock, awaiting their next adventure at sea.

PRECEDING
The guest cottage and dock of designer Steven Gambrel's home in Sag Harbor.

RIGHT
The foyer features the original nineteenth-century stair railing and wide plank floors. The wall paneling was salvaged, and the sconce was originally a fuel oil lamp from Cotswolds, England (note the small chimney).

ABOVE
The kitchen, with sweeping
views of the harbor, features
Tennessee marble floors that
were reclaimed from the
sculpture garden of the Museum
of Modern Art. The wall tiles
are from Grove Brickworks,
Steven's line for Waterworks. The
sink and counters are made of
Calacatta Paonazzo marble.

RIGHT
The breakfast room, with
access to the pool and terrace,
is furnished with a vintage
gate-leg table often used
for serving a buffet dinner
to houseguests. The second
staircase leads directly to the
master suite above.

LEFT
Steven designed the rug in the
living room to resemble
the floor planks of the home.
The sofa is vintage, and the
painting is by Josef Kugler.
The lamp on the drafting table
is by Jean-Michel Frank.

RIGHT
A smaller living room is finished
with reclaimed paneling that was
painted purple and a Belgian
writing table with vintage French
chair. The mantel is original to
the home, and the 1950s lamp is
by Jean Marais.

LEFT
The bathtub in the master suite
is from the Water Monopoly in
London. The Calacatta Paonazzo
marble used on the floors was
reclaimed from a bank.

RIGHT
A guest bedroom features a
built-in captain's bed and
fireplace. The sliding panel
adjacent to the bed reveals
a window with a view of
the harbor.

ANTIGUA
WEST INDIES

Among the Leeward Islands, in the Caribbean, is Antigua. The island is known for its sugar, corn, and sweet potato farming, as well as its fifty miles of beach and coral shoreline and the great yachting destination of English Harbour.

Designer Giorgio Armani had known Antigua well and, during a difficult time in his life, decided to buy a home there. The villa perched on the rocks, with its small, white beach below, enthralled him. Surrounded by lush tropical vegetation, the property looks out to the blue Caribbean Sea. The scenery and extraordinary colors were irresistible, and Antigua felt like an escape from the world, as island existence has its own rhythms and rituals. Island life requires authentic and unreserved contact with nature, which for Giorgio engenders a sense of boundless freedom and fulfillment.

The home, designed by Gianna Gamondi, consisted of two separate buildings with pointed roofs supported by wooden columns. Giorgio joined the two buildings, reconceived the columns, and transformed the spaces to convey the feeling of a private world that is open to the elements. His intention was to have the architecture merge naturally with the rugged, irrepressible surroundings that are in contrast to the graceful colonial architecture often found on the island.

For Giorgio, being by the sea is meditative and tranquil. Living on the water is an opportunity to explore the soul and contemplate the meaning of life. The hectic city lifestyle disappears, giving way to the natural forces of the sea.

PRECEDING
Giorgio Armani's villa in
Antigua is built into the hillside
overlooking Galley Bay and
the Caribbean Ocean. The stairs
on the right lead to a private
sandy beach.

LEFT
The multilevel villa features
numerous porches and verandas
with views of the ocean.
Louvered panels open to reveal
guest quarters.

RIGHT
A seating area was created
for optimal views of the sea.
Furnishings were designed by
Giorgio Armani.

LEFT
The dark veneered table and folding director's chairs are from Armani Casa.

RIGHT
The two adjoining villas feature pitched roofs with exposed beams. A bar nook with gray hues has seating for four guests.

IMAGES Antigua & Barbuda Alexis Andrews

LEFT
A guest bedroom with furnishings designed by Armani. The walls and floors are covered with tatami, which gives a textured aesthetic to the room.

RIGHT
The gray color palette continues into the sleek kitchen with professional stainless-steel appliances.

LEFT
Sliding louvered doors in a
bedroom offer privacy and shade
from the sun, as well as access
to the veranda overlooking
Galley Bay. The bed is from
Armani Casa.

RIGHT
A network of terraces and paths
connects the outdoor spaces,
consisting of lush tropical
gardens, swimming pools, and
a private beach.

SEAL HARBOR
MAINE

Located on Maine's remote Mount Desert Island, Seal Harbor has long been a community for "summer folk" from New York, Boston, and Philadelphia.

Much of the island had been preserved by land donated to Acadia National Park in the early 1900s by John D. Rockefeller, Jr. The pristine coastline and wooded mountains continue to make Mount Desert Island a highly desirable summer destination.

Martha Stewart had been in Maine visiting a friend, who insisted that she look at a house for sale nearby. It was a large, pink granite estate named Skylands, designed in 1925 by Duncan Candler for automotive heir Edsel Ford. Martha instantly fell in love and purchased the home.

Perched high on the land with a view of Seal Harbor, the home appealed to her because of its integration into the landscape, a testament to the original work of landscape designer Jens Jensen. There is an abundance of natural spruce, white birch, and fir trees, as well as moss-covered rocks and granite terraces that surround the home.

The house came fully furnished, even down to the Ford family's china, linens, and stemware. Martha considers herself a steward of the history and legacy of the home and its multiple outbuildings. While here she becomes immersed in all the things she loves: the outdoors, gardening, cooking, and boating. Her Hinckley motorboat *Skylands II* is docked nearby for picnic trips to the Cranberry Islands and surrounding coves with her friends and family.

PRECEDING
A view from the back terrace overlooking Seal Harbor and Little Cranberry Island. The pink granite terrace and stairs are original and lead down to the guest house and playhouse. Each Memorial Day, Martha returns her potted plants to Skylands after wintering in the greenhouse at her Bedford, New York, home.

RIGHT
The living hall is furnished with some of the many faux bois pieces that Martha has collected. The leaded glass windows are original to the home, and the telescope belonged to Edsel Ford.

Martha signed the purchase
agreement for the home on the
card table, covered with a
hand-tooled leather tablecloth.
Today it is where she and her
friends and family play Scrabble,
one of her favorite pastimes.
The stairs lead to a screening
room and wine cellar.

A view of the stair hall in the
playhouse. The turkey was a
gift from longtime friend Kevin
Sharkey, design director of
Martha Stewart. The level
below houses the squash court,
and above is the spa. The
arched doorway on the left
leads to a gallery for viewing
squash games.

The library in the main house, paneled in rich oak, houses books about Maine or written by Maine authors. As with much of the furniture in the home, the sofas and chairs belonged to the Ford family. The stained-glass lamp was made by Martha's brother.

ABOVE
The kitchen in the main house
features Pewabic tile on the
walls. The porcelain double sinks
and cypress drying racks are
original to Skylands.

RIGHT
The interior of the guest house
is painted pink, as seen here in
the living room. The table is cast
concrete, and the chairs were
upholstered in fabric by Fortuny.
The painting is by Kevin Burger.

DOMINICAN REPUBLIC

The Dominican Republic's allure is magnetic. Its white sand beaches and crystal blue waters are irresistible to visitors and those lucky enough to call this island home. New York–based editor and designer Carlos Mota had been searching for a slice of paradise near the water for his vacation house. He visited countless countries and islands but was finally sold when he visited the Dominican Republic. He felt at home in this island community, as he connected to its Latin culture, and it reminded of him of his native Venezuela.

Carlos found an isolated waterfront parcel outside of Las Terranas, which had the quiet and solitude he desired. Once he purchased the property, he began to conceptualize the home that he wanted to build. He had always admired the work of Japanese architect Tadao Ando and conceived a design using straightforward, geometric lines. Carlos chose to construct the home in concrete to best withstand the often harsh conditions of life by the ocean. He wanted a modernist feel but without a cold aesthetic. He used bold colors and textures to offset and soften the concrete, including tiles in his favorite colors of purple and lavender that he designed and had made at a local foundry in Santo Domingo. The tiles add a splash of color to the terrace, columns, and pool surround.

The home has a central courtyard, allowing expansive light into all the rooms. Carlos has collected furniture, rugs, and linens from such faraway places as Italy, Africa, and Belgium to decorate the house. The result is a vibrant and inviting seaside home and a peaceful retreat from life in New York City.

PRECEDING
The facade of Carlos Mota's home in the Dominican Republic pictured with his horse, Frederico. The house was constructed of concrete to endure the sometimes-harsh conditions near the sea.

RIGHT
Colorful cushions adorn the lounge chairs.

LEFT
Carlos designed the lavender
and purple geometric tiles on
the terrace.

ABOVE
The dining room features a
square Indonesian table; chairs
are by Frances Adler Elkins.

ABOVE
The living room is furnished
with a purple sofa covered in
striped Peruvian textiles.
The two gold chairs are by
Verner Panton. On the wall
is a rope-framed mirror
by Christian Astuguevieille.

RIGHT
The kitchen can be easily
concealed with large teak
pocket doors.

LEFT
A grouping of vintage French
mirrors is mounted above
the hollowed coral sink in the
bathroom.

ABOVE
The guest room is furnished
with art and objects from the
owner's travels.

The beach is just a few steps from the back door. The house features expansive sliding doors that open up to the view of the pool and lawn with the Caribbean Sea beyond.

224

The designer's favorite color is purple, as evidenced in a second seating area in the living room. The sofa and circular wicker seat are by Egon Eiermann. The two stools are by Hernan Arriaga, and the bull's-eye mirror is from the 1970s.

HARBOUR ISLAND
BAHAMAS

Harbour Island, located off the coast of Eleuthera in the Bahamas, is known for its pink, sandy beaches and gentle breezes. The island's history is steeped in sugar cane farming and shipbuilding.

Located in Dunmore, this four-bedroom home is a concrete structure built around an open courtyard that overlooks the turquoise blue sea. To conceive the interiors the owners brought in designer Alessandra Branca, who created a comfortable and casual home to withstand the wear and tear of sandy feet, wet towels, and salt air. Having a home herself on the island for many years has taught her that dark wood floors can be slippery, show the sand, and scratch easily. For this project she used limestone and coquina coral stone, which is durable and has a tone that relates to the sand on the beach while reflecting exterior light into the rooms. Many of the walls and vaulted ceilings are finished with pecky cypress planking, giving the rooms a relaxed and inviting feel.

Alessandra knew that the classic blue and white colors used frequently in beach homes in the northeast, where the water is much darker and better supports that color palette, would not work here. Instead she chose linen white, deep reds, and coral, which work well with the pink sand and lighter blue waters of Harbour Island.

Traditional Tahitian shutters were used on many of the exterior windows for both form and function.

When the shutters are propped up, the fixed
slats reveal the ocean view, and when returned to
the vertical position, they block the hot sun and
give the home a traditional island identity. The
kitchen features open, floating shelves and a fun
Moroccan concrete tile pattern that emulates the
waves of the sea.

PRECEDING
The view from the terrace
facing the vibrant blue ocean.

RIGHT
A sea coral theme reigns in
the living room. Clean,
contemporary slipcovered
furniture is mixed with rattan
and wicker. The walls and
vaulted ceilings are constructed
of pecky cypress paneling.
The floors are coral stone.

LEFT
A seating area with a comfortable
sectional and working privacy
shutters.

ABOVE
The dining room is beach
casual, just a few steps from the
ocean. The exterior stucco is
shell pink.

ABOVE
Alessandra commissioned the
painting from Roger Spellman
above the sofa, and the vintage
chandelier is faux coral.

RIGHT
The kitchen is finished with a
zigzag Moroccan tile designed
by Branca, inspired by waves.
The cabinets are a taupe color
to resemble driftwood.

LEFT
The bedroom features hand-embroidered bed linens and Belgian draperies. The designer found the vintage bedside chests, and the table lamps are from the 1970s.

RIGHT
The bedroom hall has a nineteenth-century Swedish daybed and a collection of eighteenth-century shell prints above. Beyond is a guest room with headboards by Alessandra in a custom Indian print.

A view of Pinks Sands Beach. The chairs and ottoman are by Restoration Hardware with fabrics by Perennials.

ACKNOWLEDGMENTS

I had the gift of being introduced to the water at a very young age, which has had a lasting impact on my life. I seem to thrive when I am in or around the water, and I am the most at ease and content.

I'd like to thank my parents, Nick and Mary Ann Voulgaris, for creating a childhood for me and my brother, Chris, that seemingly always had us near the water or out on a boat. Those early experiences helped shape my desire and need to be near the sea and to inevitably write this book.

Thank you to Charles Miers at Rizzoli, for once again entrusting me with producing a book for this iconic publishing house. Also at Rizzoli, I would like to thank my editor, Alexandra Tart, whose finesse and style always complements what I write on paper. And I would like to acknowledge Pam Sommers and Jessica Napp for all they do in promoting my projects.

I'd like to thank my friend, the photographer Douglas Friedman, for collaborating with me on this book. Doug is a modern-day Slim Aarons, and his work is the best around. Also thanks to my literary agent Carla Glasser, whose continued cheerleading keeps me signing up for more books. And thanks to Claudia Brandenburg for her elegant design.

A special thank you to Martha Stewart for writing the foreword to this book and giving us a glimpse of what it means to her to live on the water. This is the second time Martha has contributed to a book of mine, and I am grateful.

Finally, I would like to thank all of the homeowners, designers, and architects who have opened their doors to share a glimpse of what it is like to live by the sea.

Nick Voulgaris III

Whoever said writing a book was easy never photographed one. What an incredible amount of work it has been to source, gather, collect, research, and process—and what a wonderful privilege it has been to do so.

I'll try and keep this short because I'm much better with pictures than I am with words. And regarding the words, I have to thank Nick Voulgaris. It has been a thrill and a pleasure putting this book together with him. I am grateful for his input, patience, and collaborative spirit.

Speaking of patience, a big thank you to our editor, Alexandra Tart. Her guidance and dedication through the insane process of making a pretty picture book is inspired.

I would also like to thank Claudia Brandenburg for managing to find a narrative with the hundreds of pictures I dumped on her desk. Thank you for taking that task off our hands.

This book would not have been possible without the generous support of the owners of the beautiful houses featured in this book. Thank you for opening up your homes for us. It is always slightly invasive, and I appreciate your time and generosity.

And last, I want to say thank you (in no particular order) to the people who have supported me, taught me, criticized me, and encouraged me over the years. You have all had a hand in getting this book made. Thank you Carlos Mota, Cynthia Frank, Kevin Sharkey, Steven Gambrel, Michael Boodro, Ken Fulk, Robert Ruffino, Gregg Lhotsky, Kyle Lhor, my mother and father, Trey Laird, Tommy and Dee Hilfiger, Anita Sarsidi, Michael Shome, Peggy Russell, David Murphy, Luigi Menudi, Wendy Goodman, Glenda Bailey, the Culligan family, Don Burns, Amy Astley, Matthew Moneypenny, all the assistants who keep me moving forward, and, of course, my friend Martha Stewart for writing the foreword to this book.

Douglas Friedman